ASK ABOUT

ASIA

Mason Crest Publishers Inc.
370 Reed Road, Broomall, Pennsylvania 19008
(866) MCP-BOOK (toll free)
www.masoncrest.com

13 12 11 10 09 08 07 06   10 9 8 7 6 5 4 3

Library of Congress Cataloging-in-Publication Data

Hill, Valerie.
  China / [text, Valerie Hill].
     p. cm. — (Ask aboutAsia)
Summary: Explores the geography, history, people, lifestyles, and economy of China. Includes index.
     ISBN 1-59084-199-9
     ISBN 1-59084-198-0 (Series)
1. China—Juvenile literature. [1. China.] I. Title. II. Series.
951—dc21   2004297191

Printed in Malaysia.

Original concept and production by Vineyard Freepress Pty Ltd, Sydney.
Copyright © 1999 Vineyard Freepress Pty Ltd.

Project Editor	Valerie Hill
Text	Valerie Hill
Design	Denny Allnutt
Research	Peter Barker
Editor	Clare Booth
Cartography	Ray Sim
Consultant	Lynette Cunnington
Politics Adviser	Peter Coyne
Cover Design	Vineyard Freepress
Images	Mike Langford, Xinhua News Agency, Hong Kong Tourist Association, Lynette Cunnington Asian Art, Denny Allnutt, China National Tourist Office, Consulate-General of the People's Republic of China, Valerie Hill, Allan Ashby, AP/AAP, Auscape International, Sovfoto/Eastfoto, Garuda Indonesia, Pavel German, The Shanghai Museum, Peter Barker, Allen Roberts.

COVER: Traditional houses and folk dance.

TITLE PAGE: Carved and painted wooden ceiling of the Temple of Heaven, Beijing.

CONTENTS: Camels on the old Silk Road, Gansu Desert.

INTRODUCTION: New motorcycles enable young She people in remote areas to reach places of work.

China

MASON CREST PUBLISHERS

CONTENTS

MODERN CHINA

DAILY LIFE

CHINA

China is an enormous country with a great variety of landscape and climate. The third-largest country in the world (exceeded in area only by Russia and Canada), China occupies most of the eastern part of the mainland of Asia. From its western border to the eastern seacoast, the country is 3,125 miles (5,000 kilometers) wide. Most of China is mountainous, and 90 percent of its vast population lives in only 20 percent of its land—mainly in the fertile coastal regions of the east and south. The Changjiang (Yangtze River), the largest in China, divides the country into north and south. The mighty Huanghe (Yellow River) takes its name from the yellow soil that colors its waters as they flow through northern China.

China's wildlife includes the golden-haired monkey, the red-crowned crane, and the giant panda, an endangered species found only in bamboo forests in the south. There are more than 2,000 edible plants and some of the world's richest mineral reserves.

CLIMATE

China has a continental monsoon climate with the widest climatic range in the world. There are great differences in temperature and rainfall—from bitterly cold winters in Tibet and the north, to the humid year-round tropical conditions of the extreme south and southeast. The east coast where most people live is warm and humid, with four distinct seasons.

CENTRAL ASIA

Tian Shan

Turpan Depression

C   H

Kunlun Shan

Qinghai-Tibet Plateau

TIBET

Himalayas

Qomolangma (Mount Everest)   Lhasa

FACT FILE

Official Name: People's Republic of China
Official Language: Mandarin Chinese
Population: 1,300,000,000
Capital: Beijing (Population: 12,510,000)
Currency: *Yuan* (Y)
Land Area: 6,000,000 sq miles (9,600,000 sq km)
Ethnic Groups: Han 92%; Chuang 1.4%; Manchu 0.9%; Hui 0.8%; Miao 0.7%; Uygur 0.6%; Yi 0.6%; Tuchia 0.5%; Mongolian 0.4%; Tibetan 0.4%; Others 1.7%
Religions: Nonreligious 71.2%; Chinese Folk Religion 20.1%; Buddhist 6%; Muslim 2.4%; Christian 0.2%; Other 0.1%
Major Physical Features: Highest mountain: Mount Qomolangma (Mount Everest) 29,029 ft (8,848 m); Longest river: Changjiang 3,915 miles (6,300 km); Lowest point: Turpan Depression –505 ft (–154 m) below sea level

MODERN CHINA

DAILY LIFE

INTRODUCTION

ONE QUARTER of the world's people live in China, a vast, diverse country of the Asian continent. Its ancient civilization emerged from farming villages along rivers and grew from small kingdoms into the present immense nation of 56 ethnic groups. Believing their own culture to be superior to the outside world, the Chinese developed a unique way of life and thought. Their language, writing, art, food, and farming influenced many other Asian cultures.

Twentieth-century China experienced the turbulence of revolution when its traditional dynastic system was overthrown. In the new era, under communism, young Chinese people are faced with a mixture of ideas—ancient and modern, eastern and western—and they now have a growing awareness of the rest of the world.

CHINA

China is an enormous country with a great variety of landscape and climate. The third-largest country in the world (exceeded in area only by Russia and Canada), China occupies most of the eastern part of the mainland of Asia. From its western border to the eastern seacoast, the country is 3,125 miles (5,000 kilometers) wide. Most of China is mountainous, and 90 percent of its vast population lives in only 20 percent of its land—mainly in the fertile coastal regions of the east and south. The Changjiang (Yangtze River), the largest in China, divides the country into north and south. The mighty Huanghe (Yellow River) takes its name from the yellow soil that colors its waters as they flow through northern China.

China's wildlife includes the golden-haired monkey, the red-crowned crane, and the giant panda, an endangered species found only in bamboo forests in the south. There are more than 2,000 edible plants and some of the world's richest mineral reserves.

CLIMATE

China has a continental monsoon climate with the widest climatic range in the world. There are great differences in temperature and rainfall—from bitterly cold winters in Tibet and the north, to the humid year-round tropical conditions of the extreme south and southeast. The east coast where most people live is warm and humid, with four distinct seasons.

CENTRAL ASIA

Tian Shan

Turpan Depression

C   H

Kunlun Shan

Qinghai-Tibet Plateau

TIBET

Himalayas

Qomolangma (Mount Everest)   Lhasa

FACT FILE

Official Name: People's Republic of China
Official Language: Mandarin Chinese
Population: 1,300,000,000
Capital: Beijing (Population: 12,510,000)
Currency: *Yuan* (Y)
Land Area: 6,000,000 sq miles (9,600,000 sq km)
Ethnic Groups: Han 92%; Chuang 1.4%; Manchu 0.9%; Hui 0.8%; Miao 0.7%; Uygur 0.6%; Yi 0.6%; Tuchia 0.5%; Mongolian 0.4%; Tibetan 0.4%; Others 1.7%
Religions: Nonreligious 71.2%; Chinese Folk Religion 20.1%; Buddhist 6%; Muslim 2.4%; Christian 0.2%; Other 0.1%
Major Physical Features: Highest mountain: Mount Qomolangma (Mount Everest) 29,029 ft (8,848 m); Longest river: Changjiang 3,915 miles (6,300 km); Lowest point: Turpan Depression –505 ft (–154 m) below sea level

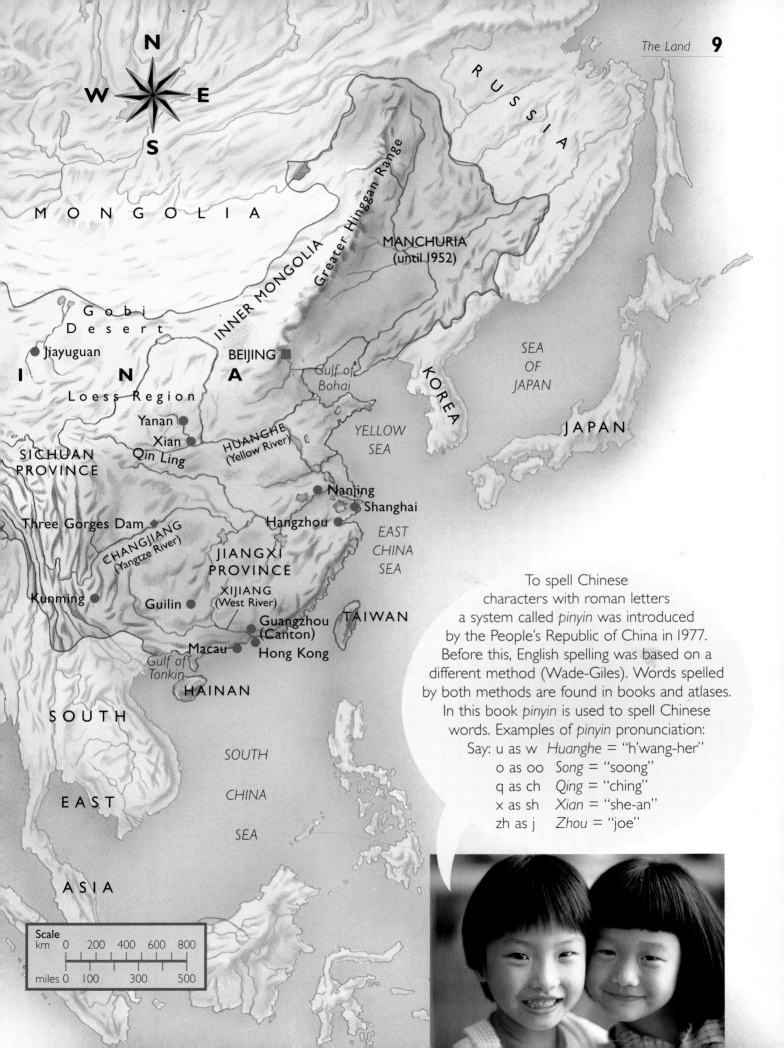

N
W • E
S

RUSSIA

MONGOLIA

Greater Hinggan Range

MANCHURIA
(until 1952)

INNER MONGOLIA

Gobi
Desert

Jiayuguan

BEIJING ■

Gulf of
Bohai

SEA
OF
JAPAN

KOREA

JAPAN

I   N   A

Loess Region

Yanan

Xian

Qin Ling

HUANGHE
(Yellow River)

YELLOW
SEA

SICHUAN
PROVINCE

Nanjing
Shanghai

Three Gorges Dam

CHANGJIANG
(Yangtze River)

Hangzhou

EAST
CHINA
SEA

JIANGXI
PROVINCE

Kunming

XIJIANG
(West River)

Guilin

TAIWAN

Guangzhou
(Canton)

Macau

Hong Kong

Gulf of
Tonkin

HAINAN

SOUTH

EAST

SOUTH

CHINA

ASIA

SEA

To spell Chinese
characters with roman letters
a system called *pinyin* was introduced
by the People's Republic of China in 1977.
Before this, English spelling was based on a
different method (Wade-Giles). Words spelled
by both methods are found in books and atlases.
In this book *pinyin* is used to spell Chinese
words. Examples of *pinyin* pronunciation:
Say: u as w   *Huanghe* = "h'wang-her"
o as oo   *Song* = "soong"
q as ch   *Qing* = "ching"
x as sh   *Xian* = "she-an"
zh as j   *Zhou* = "joe"

Scale
km 0   200   400   600   800
miles 0   100   300   500

GREAT MOUNTAINS AND RIVERS

China's landscape is dominated by mountains and shaped by rivers. From the backdrop of the mighty Himalayas along its southwest border, the land falls in three great uneven steps from the Qinghai-Tibet Plateau in the west to the eastern seacoast. Rain and melting snow drain from the mountains into 50,000 rivers, which begin as fast-flowing streams, carrying fertile soil to the plains below, where they spread and meander. Wind and mountains also interact to bring climatic changes. China's three great steps, with their different mountain, river, and plain landscapes, are shown in the diagram below.

▲ Within the Himalayas Qomolangma (Mount Everest) is 29,029 ft (8,848 m) above sea level.

1 QINGHAI-TIBET PLATEAU averages 12,120 feet (4,000 meters) above sea level. The highest step of China's topography is the Qinghai-Tibet Plateau, known as "the roof of the world." It is a cold, dry wilderness with rarefied air.

2 LOWER MOUNTAIN RANGES, PLATEAUX AND DESERT REGIONS 3,030–6,060 ft (1,000–2,000 m) above sea level. The land falls from the wide second level, through lower mountain ranges, grass-covered tablelands, and dry inland deserts. In the northeast heavily forested mountains divide the interior from the coastal region.

▲ Sheep graze on the Tibetan Plateau near Lhasa during the short summer (Step 1).

▶ A fast-running stream of rain and melted snow from the high mountains (Step 1) has cut a gorge through a valley near Kunming (Step 2).

▼ The Lijiang flows between worn limestone mountains near Guilin into the Xijiang, a deep, busy shipping route to the city of Guangzhou (Step 3).

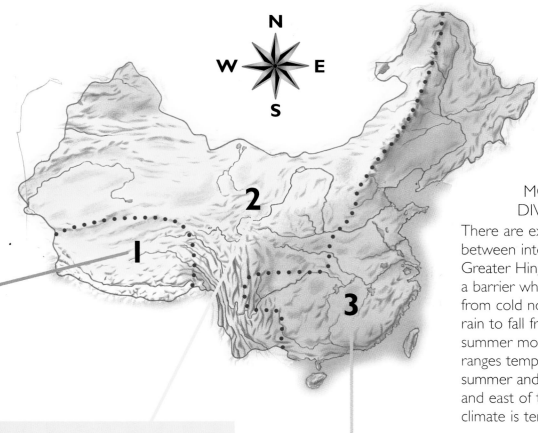

MOUNTAINS THAT DIVIDE THE CLIMATE

There are extreme variations of climate between interior and coastal China—the Greater Hinggan and Qilian Ranges form a barrier which protects the coastal areas from cold north winds. The ranges cause rain to fall from the southerly humid summer monsoons. Northwest of the ranges temperatures are extremely hot in summer and bitterly cold in winter. South and east of this mountain barrier the climate is temperate to tropical all year.

3 **FERTILE COASTAL PLAINS**
1,515–3,030 ft (500–1,000 m) above sea level.
To the south and east, the third step descends to hills and coastal plains—the "food bowl"—with deep fertile soil built up by river silt. Paddy fields are irrigated with water from the many rivers.

◄ A watercourse in the Turpan Depression. Waters flowing inland in the north and west areas of Step 2 disappear into deserts or form lakes.

◄ Paddy fields in the southeast of Steps 2 and 3 utilize water and rich silt deposits to grow rice.

► The Changjiang (Yangtze) is China's longest river. It forms lakes and a great delta before emptying into the East China Sea near the city of Shanghai. Seagoing ships navigate inland as far as Sichuan. (Steps 1–2–3–4).

EARLY CIVILIZATION

The valley of the Huanghe (Yellow River) is often called the "cradle of Chinese civilization." Here the nation began in small settlements where farmers grew millet, wheat, and barley in the rich soil, while in the warmer southern valley of the Changjiang (Yangtze River), cultivation of rice began. Daily life was based on beliefs that heaven controlled rain, drought, and flood, so great efforts were made to please unseen gods and ward off evil spirits. If crops failed, people went hungry, and a leader who did not appear to protect his people from natural disasters lost his right to rule.

▲ Pictographs, an early form of writing, were carved on bones and pottery to be used in rituals seeking guidance for the future.

▼ During the last 50 years archaeologists have found many artefacts in sites of early settlement in the river valleys.

▲ Using a waterwheel to supply irrigation channels, farmers increased rice yields by growing the young plants in flooded paddy fields divided by low mud walls which held the water.

Since the twenty-first century BC China's history has been measured by "dynasty"—a period ruled continuously by generations of the same family. Many dynasties were overthrown after members became weak or corrupt. When rulers died, the precious objects placed in their tombs often became the only lasting records of these early kingdoms.

▶ A *ding*, or bronze cauldron, was used by the wandering Zhou (pronounced "joe") who overthrew the Shang in about 1100 BC and dominated other states. The Zhou Dynasty called themselves "Sons of Heaven" and claimed a mandate, or right to rule. Their weapons and tools were iron, and they used slaves to build extensive water control systems.

▲ Bronze *wenyigong*, or wine jug, of the Shang dynasty, which seized power about 1480 BC. During its rule, silk was woven, wheeled chariots were used, and a form of writing was developed.

▲ The *yin-yang* symbol from the ancient "Way of Tao" (Dow) represents a Chinese view of the balance of forces in people and the universe.

▲ In the Warring States period (475–221 BC) the dragon was a symbol of water, rain and the sea. The Dragon Throne represented imperial power. Warlords ruled their own kingdoms and enlarged their constant battles by gathering armies of peasants. They also built walls from which their armies could repel invaders.

▶ Kingdoms had their own coins of different shapes, such as this bronze "knife money."

CONFUCIANISM

China's great philosopher Confucius (551–497 BC) lived in a turbulent era. He sought a more peaceful way of life and taught that rulers should be honorable and sincere, subjects should be loyal, scholars honest, and that the young should respect their elders. Strict rules were developed setting out the right way to behave for people of all classes. The high honor given to ancestors became central to the Chinese way of life and worship.

FROM FIRST EMPEROR TO THE HAN

The "Tiger of Qin" (pronounced "chin"), with fierce mounted archers and battering rams, defeated the other Warring States and formed them into an empire. In 221 BC he proclaimed himself *Shi huangdi*—"First Emperor" of Qin—and for the next 2,000 years China's rulers took the title Emperor. Qin Shihuangdi centralized and controlled his empire by imposing standard systems of law, money, weights, and measures, and building a network of roads. Walls built by the Warring States were connected to prevent "barbarians" entering the farmlands. But farms were neglected while 300,000 people worked on the walls, so it was famine and the rebellion of Qin Shihuangdi's own people that brought his dynasty to an end.

▲ Qin Shihuangdi died in 207 BC. His tomb was like a strange underworld with a jewelled sky and rivers of mercury. Thousands of life-size terracotta warriors and horses were placed in its entrance corridors.

◄ The writing system standardized during the Qin Dynasty has changed little since that time. To prevent the spread of earlier philosophies and ideas different from his own, the Emperor had scholars killed and their books burned.

CHINA'S NAMES
The Chinese considered their civilization to be unique and surrounded by barbarians. They therefore called it *Chung-kuo*, or "Middle Country," often translated as "Middle Kingdom." *Chung-kuo* is still the Chinese name for their land, while the western word "China" is taken from the Qin Dynasty, which first unified the country.

▶ Bronze container for tributes— payments from other countries which submitted to China. It dates from the Han period and contained cowrie shells, which were used as currency as far away as Africa.

A strong rebel general, Liu Bang, founded the Han
Dynasty, which ruled for 430 years (209 BC to AD 220).
The next emperor, Wu Ti, enlarged the Han Empire,
which became as significant in the east as the Roman
Empire was in the west. Most Chinese still identify
themselves as "people of the Han." The empire was
organized according to the teachings of Confucius,
whose ideas remained influential until the twentieth century.
Paper replaced wood, bamboo, and silk as a writing material. Books
of legends and histories of past dynasties were written and circulated.
After the fall of the Han, China split into many small kingdoms,
until reunited by the Sui Dynasty.

▲ Gold inlaid copper
tiger with an
inscription about
raising a troop.
Han Dynasty.

◀ Comb box of
red lacquerware.
Its fine surface
was produced by applying
hundreds of layers of Rhus tree
sap to a wood or cloth base.

THE GREAT TRADE ROUTES

An ancient trade route linked Han Dynasty China in the east
with the Roman Empire in the west. Caravans of camels
carried Chinese silk, ivory, plants, and paper, and returned with
horses, gold, silver, glass, and sandalwood. The loads were
transferred in relays, and took up to one year to travel from China to the Mediterranean Sea. This route,
later known as the Silk Road, was 4,375 miles (7,000 kilometers) long, and skirted deserts and high
mountain ranges. It was no longer safe to use after the collapse of the Roman Empire.

Sea routes were established during the first century AD when ships traveled south with the monsoon winds
to India and returned with the next monsoon. These traders brought luxury goods, different cultures, and
new ideas, including Buddhism from India. Tropical diseases of smallpox and bubonic plague also entered
the country and infected the Chinese,
who had no resistance.

◀ Grapes were among the earliest plants
carried into China along the Silk Road.
Roses, dates, nuts, peaches, and pears
came from Persia (Iran), cucumbers
and onions from Central Asia.

THE TANG AND SONG

During the golden age of the Tang Dynasty trade, business and the arts flourished. Over 70 million people lived in the empire, the largest state of that period. The capital Xian, starting point for Silk Road caravans, attracted scholars and merchants from as far away as Arabia, Africa, Persia, Korea, and Japan. The city had districts for different classes of people, walls with gates that were locked at night, houses with curved tiled roofs, and beautiful gardens. People, especially landowners, began to live in cities and towns, in which amusements, tea shops, and restaurants flourished. Following the collapse of the Tang Dynasty in AD 907, China was divided under different rulers.

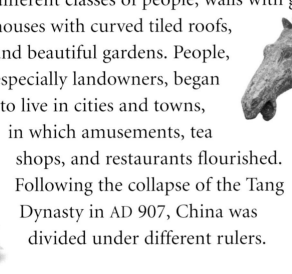

▲ Pottery figure from the Tang Court.

▶ Horses were admired and valued. This Tang Dynasty painted pottery horse once had a mane and tail of real hair.

▲
A straw and stucco Buddha 89 feet (27 meters) tall marks the Binglingsi Caves. They were carved into cliff walls of the Huanghe before AD 500.

BUDDHISM

Buddhism had a great impact on Chinese civilization and influenced artistic expression, especially writing, the arts, and architecture. Different forms of Buddhism existed in China. Followers sought *Nirvana* —a state of heavenly bliss—which they hoped to achieve through ritual, meditation, and a cycle of countless rebirths in different forms.

▶ Because he believed that even an ant or beetle might be a reborn soul, the monk Xuan Zang hung a small bell from his carrying frame to warn them of his approach. Xuan is famous for his 15,625-mile (25,000-kilometer) journey to bring Buddhist scriptures from India to China. He traveled for 17 years and took a further 20 years to translate the Sanskrit into Chinese.

The Song Dynasty (AD 960–1279) reunited the country in a period rich in poetry, painting, and calligraphy. Scholars, artists, and scientists were encouraged, and education spread to middle-class merchants and craftsmen. Paper money was used for the first time; gunpowder was made, and tea became popular. There were many technological advances during the Song Dynasty, and China went through a minor industrial revolution. Iron ore was mined and smelted for tools, weapons, nails, and coins; compasses were invented, and salt was mined and taken to the furthest parts of the empire on a network of roads and canals.

▲ Hand-held scales weigh items by balancing a sliding weight along a graduated rod.

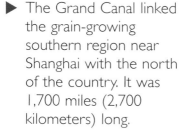

◀ An abacus, the first calculator.

▶ The Grand Canal linked the grain-growing southern region near Shanghai with the north of the country. It was 1,700 miles (2,700 kilometers) long.

WRITING

Moveable print and block printing were developed by the eighth century, so textbooks and scrolls could be printed easily and used widely. Calligraphy, poetry, and painting were known as the "three perfections," and brush pens were used on silk and paper.

▶ Flowing style of calligraphy by Su Shi, a famous poet of the Song period.

▶ Modern brushes, paper, ink, and inkstone are still described as "the four treasures of the scholar's studio."

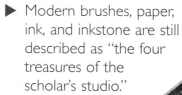

FROM MONGOLS TO THE MING

During the thirteenth century AD, fierce hordes of Mongol horsemen, led by Chinggis (Genghis) Khan, rampaged through Central Asia. His grandson Kubilai Khan conquered northern China and established the Yuan Dynasty with its capital at Khanbaliq (now Beijing). For almost one hundred years China was part of the vast Mongol Empire, which stretched as far as eastern Europe. The Silk Road, within Mongol territory, was reopened, and Marco Polo made his fabled visit to the Great Khan. Drama flourished in cities, and novels developed from the tales of storytellers. Weak Mongol leaders were overthrown by the Chinese Ming Dynasty.

▲ Mongol warrior.

◀ Many Muslim regions were conquered by the Mongols and have remained part of China. There are now 20 million Muslims in China, mostly centered in the northwestern provinces.

▼ The Great Wall, the only architectural structure in the world that can be seen from space, was completed during the Ming Dynasty's 300-year rule. Walls built by earlier rulers as far back as the fifth century BC were linked to make the Great Wall, which runs nearly 4,000 miles (6,000 kilometers) across north China, from Jiayuguan in the west to the Yellow Sea in the east.

A ceramic sedan chair with bearers. Veils hid the person being carried, whose rank was shown by color. Only the imperial family used yellow. Traditionally, brides were carried to their husband's house in a sealed red chair. The Ming Dynasty is famous for ceramics.

▲ Ming Dynasty costume. (Palace Museum, Beijing.)

When the Ming dynasty restored Chinese control in AD 1368, it began 276 years of peace. Besides encouraging literature and the arts, early emperors reduced taxes and improved irrigation and agriculture. Great architectural landmarks built by the Ming include the Forbidden City and the Great Wall. Treasure ships sailed south, and for the first time, Europeans came to China by sea. From the mid-sixteenth century China was a rich society, but it kept to traditional ways while Europe was experiencing the dynamic changes of the Renaissance and Reformation. Later weak emperors and corrupt court officials were destroyed, not by outside attackers but by rebel bands of Chinese.

▼ Huge stone sculptures of animals, including camels, elephants, and lions, guard the avenue leading to the tombs where the Ming emperors were buried.

◄ Admiral Zheng He sailed on seven voyages of discovery, passing through the Malacca Strait to India, the Persian Gulf, and Africa. On the first voyage in AD 1405–07 there were over 300 ships in the fleet. Several treasure ships were over 400 ft (122 m) long. They had watertight compartments to keep them afloat, and were navigated with magnetic compasses. On board were vegetable gardens and live animals for supplies.

QING—THE LAST DYNASTY

Manchus from the northeast overran the Great Wall, marched on the Forbidden City and established the Qing ("ching") Dynasty in AD 1644. Manchu emperors maintained the style and refinement of the court, clinging to the old ways of the Ming Dynasty. China considered its own culture to be superior and, like its neighbors Korea and Japan, closed its doors to foreigners. Meanwhile, European nations experienced an Age of Discovery, and surged forward in science and technology. During the seventeenth and eighteenth centuries they came to China in search of trade and dominions, bringing missionaries with them. There were vast differences between the way of thinking of the Chinese, who valued tradition, and the Europeans, who valued progress.

▲ Manchu emperors retained the Chinese mandarins as court administrators, but made them show submission by shaving their heads and wearing a long pigtail at the back.

▲ The imperial dragon
◄ is emblazoned on fine porcelain dishes. On the underside is the seal (or mark) of the Emperor Jiaqing (1796–1820).

THE COMING OF THE WEST

The earliest Europeans to trade with China were the Portuguese and Dutch. Merchants of the British East India Company, wanting to buy tea, silk, and porcelain, offered woolen cloth and manufactured goods. But the Emperor wrote to Britain's King George III that China "does not attach great importance to strange and clever objects, and has no need of your manufactured products." The Company then began to supply the drug opium. More and more Chinese became addicted, leading to the Opium Wars between China and Britain. British victories gained trade rights, and, soon after, other European nations claimed similar rights.

▲ A children's book written in both Chinese and English, but read from right to left, describes tea growing, c.1900.

► Shanghai was made one of several Treaty Ports, where Western and Japanese residences and trading posts were built. On its famous waterfront avenue, The Bund, many grand colonial buildings still stand. Transport systems were developed, and the small island of Hong Kong, with its deep harbor, was handed over to Britain, which developed it as a leader in world trade and business.

◀ Door of Hope bride doll. Her traditional Chinese wedding dress was sewn by a girl in the Door of Hope Mission, Shanghai, a safe house for destitute girls. Established in 1901 by five Christian women, it gave the girls a home and schooling, and taught them to sew. The dolls in authentic dress—families, farmers, mandarins—are still collected and treasured worldwide.

▲ The Manchus retained court dances, but kept their own identity by changing dress styles from the long Chinese robe to the jacket, wide trousers, and boots suited to riding.

▼ The Qing conquered neighboring peoples such as the Uygurs, who remain part of China. They herd sheep and lead a nomadic life, moving their portable *yurts*.

Later, palace waste and neglect of important works allowed silt in the Grand Canal to slow grain transport; dikes which carried the Huanghe above ground level were not maintained, so the great river broke loose and changed course. Flood was followed by famine, and thousands of peasants died. A great anger turned to violence, and from 1850 there were rebellions until finally the 1911 Revolution brought down the Qing dynasty and ended 2,000 years of imperial rule.

▶

The little Emperor Pu Yi was only six years old when the Qing Dynasty came to an end. A scene from *The Last Emperor*, a film by Bernardo Bertolucci, shows him in the Forbidden City, where he was allowed to remain until 1924.

THE PEOPLE REVOLT

Far-reaching revolution ended imperial rule in China at the beginning of the twentieth century. Its causes included increased population, poverty, and famine in the countryside and discontent among city dwellers, unfair taxes, a corrupt court, and the presence of foreigners. Secret societies plotted against the imperial Manchu court until the 1911 Revolution forced the last emperor to abdicate. A Chinese Republic was declared. Under the leadership of Yuan Shihkai, hopes for a democratic government were destroyed.

Instead, a destructive power struggle between warlords began. Japanese aggression in Manchuria sparked widespread Chinese protest, remembered as the 1919 "May 4th Movement." Protesters carried banners saying "Save the Country," reflecting a growing nationalism. In 1921 the Communist Party of China was formed with 57 members. (By 1993 it had grown to 57 million members.)

▲ At the end of the Qing Dynasty, peasants had so little land and had to give so much of their crops to landlords that they starved in times of drought and flood. In city factories, poorly paid workers toiled under bad conditions seven days a week.

▲ Dr. Sun Yat Sen, called the father of the revolution, led the early movement toward a Chinese republic.

▲ Traditional clothes of the imperial era were decorated with symbols to show the rank of the wearer and to bring good fortune. The crane symbolizes majesty, wisdom, and long life, the wave pattern immortality.

IMPERIAL DRESS

▼ Women's feet in tiny embroidered shoes were considered beautiful, so from about three years old a girl's four smaller toes were bent and tightly bound with cloth strips to stunt her foot to about 3 inches (7.5 cm) long. This inflicted great pain and made walking almost impossible, but wealthy men did not want to marry a woman whose feet were unbound.

▲ Embroidered squares showed status. Military ranks featured animals on their insignia.

Communists and Nationalists joined forces to defeat the warlords. Afterward, the Nationalists, led by Jiang Jieshi (Chiang Kaishek), turned on the Communists. Surrounded, they retreated into the mountains and began the famous Long March, which has become part of communist folklore. During this ordeal, Mao Zedong became leader of the Red Army. The year-long march ended in 1935 when a safe northern base was established in the caves of Yanan. Communist influence grew as they and the Nationalists fought against Japanese occupation of China, which was ended only by the defeat of Japan in 1945, at the end of World War II. On 1 October 1949, Mao Zedong proclaimed the People's Republic of China. The Nationalists fled to Taiwan, claiming that theirs was the real government of China (a claim still maintained today). China had undergone tumultuous change—after nearly forty years of conflict, following the end of the imperial age, the communist era was begun.

▲ On the Long March, 100,000 men and women crossed snowy mountains, rivers, and treacherous marshes—a 6,000-mile (9,600-km) journey from Jiangxi to Yanan. They were often hungry and under Nationalist attack. Only one in five survived the ordeal, but they became heroes, and because they did not rob or abuse the people along the way, many followed them.

▲ Red, the color of revolution, is worn on uniforms or armbands and displayed in flags, banners, and badges. The large yellow star stands for the Communist Party of China.

COMMUNIST DRESS

▶ Communist revolutionaries, both men and women, officers and soldiers, wore plain unfitted jackets and trousers in hardwearing khaki or dark blue fabric. This made them appear equal and part of the group. The style, *zhong-shan zhuang*, first made popular by Sun Yat Sen, imitated the uniforms of the Russian revolutionary army. Red flashes and a star on the cap identify soldiers.

▲ Huge posters of Chairman Mao were part of Communist Party propaganda.

MAO ZEDONG THOUGHT

The Communist Party of China (CPC) had begun under guidance from Russia and the thoughts of the two founders of modern communism, Marx and Lenin. The CPC broke away from Soviet ideas and added the thoughts of Mao Zedong, which became a cult of liberation for the Chinese peasant. Liberation was taught by party workers sent to live, work, and eat in the villages with the peasants. Communist doctrine was even taught in art forms such as folk song and dance, and prints and paintings of communal workers.
Liberation meant CPC dictatorship:

- Revolution aimed to give the masses a new life by overturning old ideas about government, private property, law;
- this could be achieved only under the total power of a centralized party with a strong army;
- members submitted to absolute CPC discipline, acting not as individuals but as part of the group.

MAO AND COMMUNISM

Mao Zedong was already a hero to many Chinese before he became leader in 1949. His purpose was to form a new society in which workers and peasants would take control from the upper classes. But before this could happen, Mao said, there would be conflict, class struggle, and further revolution. When the new communist government took over, it stripped landlords of their property and forced land redistribution, made women equal with men, sent children to school, and put most adults to work. It also controlled every person's life. At first things seemed better, but production was low. An experiment called the Great Leap Forward tried to speed progress using the physical labor of 100 million men and women. Between 1958 and 1960, peasants lived in communes, and children were cared for by old people, while the men and women toiled on massive rural projects.

▲ Workers haul rocks for water control systems along the Huanghe during the Great Leap Forward. Urged on by propaganda, they tried with all their strength, but goals set by the government kept increasing and could not be achieved. Many workers died from disease and famine after crops failed due to poor planning and inexperience, drought and flood.

◀ In this painting, titled *Condemning Confucius at His Temple Gate*, by Chao Kun-han, the speaker and crowd cheer communism and shout slogans against old ways and beliefs.

By 1966, Mao Zedong, afraid that his ideas of revolution were being changed, told young people that it was right to rebel. Universities and schools were forced to close and the Cultural Revolution took over. Young Red Guards attacked the "four olds"—old ideas, old culture, old customs, and old habits. Educated people such as doctors, teachers, musicians, their families, and even old soldiers of the Long March were jeered at, beaten, and sometimes killed. During "Ten Years of Chaos," the army took control, and 18 million young people were "sent down" to the countryside to teach and learn from the peasants, while some officials were "reeducated" in hard-labor camps. Since Mao Zedong died in 1976, other leaders have shaped and adjusted communism in China, but "Mao Zedong thought" remains part of the Constitution.

▲ Cultural Revolution parade of Red Guards, who attacked "wrong thinking." They hold the "little red book," *Thoughts of Chairman Mao*, which they memorized and obeyed. It became famous overseas.

◀ A statue, in the idealized social realist style, shows Mao as a kind of savior of the people, or father of the nation as he is remembered, although the revolution brought both advances and disasters. Every year, thousands of Chinese pay their respects to his body, preserved in its mausoleum in Beijing.

National emblem of the People's Republic of China. The color red symbolizes revolution; Tiananmen Gate, the unyielding spirit of the people; the cogwheel, the workers; grain, the peasants; the large star, the CPC; and the small stars, the people under the Communist Party.

GOVERNMENT AND PEOPLES

Since 1949 China has been a communist republic, which, the Constitution says, is ruled as a "democratic dictatorship." Government structure has three major parts, each with a number of powerful committees, and each connected with the others:

The Communist Party of China (CPC) controls every aspect of society. It lays down policies and has branches everywhere in China. There is no opposition party. Other minor parties support the CPC.

The National People's Congress (NPC) is made up of 3,000 members elected from regions. They meet once a year to discuss and accept policies and laws proposed by the Party. Permanent committees and departments carry out government decisions.

The People's Liberation Army (PLA) is controlled by both Party and Congress. Soldiers have a high status and many join the CPC.

DEMOCRATIC DICTATORSHIP

In politics, the word "democratic" usually means the opposite of "dictatorship," but the Chinese Constitution explains it as "democracy within the ranks of the people and dictatorship over the enemies of the people." Which word applies is determined by the Four Cardinal Principles that every person and every political party must obey:
• follow the "socialist road"
• follow the people's democratic dictatorship
• follow the leadership of the Communist Party
• follow Marxism-Leninism and Mao Zedong thought.

"Democracy," where people or groups express opinions and make decisions, can be practiced so long as they obey the Four Cardinal Principles.

"Dictatorship" comes into action when a person or group fails to follow the Four Cardinal Principles—they are then "traitors, counter-revolutionaries, and criminals" and are severely punished. For example, in 1989 when student demonstrators in Beijing protested against Party policies they were treated as "traitors, counter-revolutionaries, and criminals" and the army used tanks and guns against them and imprisoned many of their leaders.

References pp. 26–27: *China*, an official government handbook, New Star Publishers, Beijing, 1997.

▲ President Jiang Zemin with representatives of Macau, a former treaty port that was returned to China in 1999.

▼ China's unit of money is the *yuan*. The currency is called *renminbi*, meaning "the people's money."

GENERAL GUIDE TO RULING BODIES OF THE PEOPLE'S REPUBLIC OF CHINA

Note: there are many committees and related organizations not shown here.

COMMUNIST PARTY OF CHINA
Makes policies
POLITBURO (Political bureau)
The most influential decision-making body
CENTRAL COMMITTEE
Made up of CPC leaders,
controls local branches

PEOPLE'S LIBERATION ARMY
Has a high budget
and is controlled
directly by the CPC
and the NPC

NATIONAL PEOPLE'S CONGRESS
Implements laws according to CPC
policies. Representatives are elected.
Other elected parties work with the
CPC to report people's opinions
and supervize the CPC's work.
There is no opposition party.

**COURTS, POLICE, PARTY BRANCHES, BUREAUCRACY,
WORK UNITS, AND STREET COMMITTEES**

Decisions made by the Communist Party are carried through its members to branches
in all regions. Laws passed by the National Congress are put into action by the legal
system, police, and work or school units. Street committees oversee the day-to-day
running of their areas. Permission must be sought for such things as changing houses
or jobs, getting married, or having a baby. They also organize services such as child care,
and deal with problems and lawbreakers at the local level.

▲ The army has always
had a key role in
CPC structure.

▼ Young people on
volunteer traffic
duty during their
school vacation.

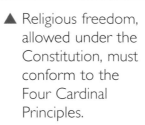

▲ Religious freedom,
allowed under the
Constitution, must
conform to the
Four Cardinal
Principles.

▼ Every youth group
is part of the
All-China Youth
Federation, under
the CPC Central
Committee.

▲ A voluntary advisor
writes a blackboard
newspaper. He
works with a street
committee leader,
who supervises
everything in her
street.

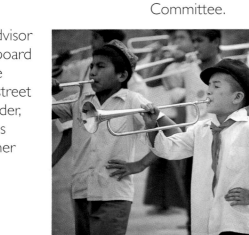

CHINA AND OTHER COUNTRIES

Ancient China influenced neighboring countries in their earliest periods—much of its culture was absorbed by Korea and Japan, and waves of Chinese migrated to South East Asia. Much later, in the nineteenth-century gold rushes, Chinese came to Australia, Canada, and the United States. Many who live abroad to study or work have made significant contributions to their adopted countries—in business, medicine, science, music—and their children have grown up as citizens. Some are now returning to China to use their knowledge and experience in the new economic development, which began in the late 1970s. At that time, the Chinese government "opened its doors" to welcome foreign tourism, sports, manufacture, and trade.

▲ "Long March" carrier rockets have launched 53 satellites for the international commercial launching market.

◄ Students from Hong Kong at an Australian boarding school are among the many who study overseas. Some parents buy a house near their chosen school.

▲ Gifts of money in red envelopes are given at Chinese New Year with traditional wishes for good luck, happiness, and long life. Each year in a twelve-year cycle is represented by an animal: for example, Year of the Pig, Year of the Tiger.

▼ The crowded Shanghai Stock Exchange is busy with trade in both local and international stocks and shares.

▲ Chinese medicine, which uses plants, herbs, and dried animal material, is used by people in many countries.

◀ Early morning groups practise *Tai Chi* exercises in parks wherever there are Chinese communities. Other forms of exercise and martial arts are increasingly popular in other countries.

Wherever they go, the Chinese take their language, customs, food, and medicine—and their ability to make money. The countries they adopt often have two opposing attitudes to Chinese immigrants. They are sought after for their skills and hardworking habits but are sometimes rejected because their willing work and business success make many of them richer and more powerful than the local people.

▲ Bronze statues of Buddha made in China are sold to other countries for use in Buddhist temples.

◀ Chinese calligraphy, the art of writing, has become one of the world's great art forms. It is admired for its fluent strength and style even when the meaning is not understood. The character shown here means "Buddha."

▼ Colorful and noisy, dragon boat races, lion dances, and New Year fireworks are part of displays and celebrations in many countries where Chinese have settled.

▲ After international complaints of pirating, Chinese authorities burned 120,000 pirated CD-ROMs in 1996. New laws to protect trademarks and copyright bear heavy punishments for offenders.

AGRICULTURE

China is the world's leading producer of wheat and rice. Corn is also a major grain crop. Large fields in the northern wheat belts are farmed with tractors, while south of the Changjiang, machinery and water buffaloes work flooded paddy fields. Other crops include barley, sweet potatoes, sesame (for oil), cotton, maize, sugar cane, and tobacco. With only one-third of the land suitable for farming, careful management is essential. Over half of China's people were exclusively farmers until moves to set up local industries, such as clothing and food processing factories, in rural towns.

▲ Rice is generally grown in the warmer south.

FARMING FISH AND ANIMALS

Fish are raised in large fish farms. Pigs, ducks, and chickens are important for food. In the dry northwestern grasslands, with bitterly cold winters, sheep, cattle, goats, and horses are grazed.

▼ "White Gold." Cotton growers in Xinjiang sell their produce.

In southern subtropical areas with high rainfall, there is a twelve-month growing season that can often produce two rice crops, a winter crop of beans or peanuts, and tropical fruits, including bananas, mangoes, citrus, lychees, melons, and pineapples. Collective farming has been adapted to allow farmers to fill a quota and sell surplus at a local market. Agricultural science and technology is increasing production with new strains of vegetables, grains and livestock, but farming still needs further mechanization.

▲ A wide range of fresh vegetables is grown for sale in local markets.

▲ Traditional farmer in flooded paddy field. These must be level, so paddy fields on slopes are terraced.

◄ Different forms of transport work side by side—horse-drawn carts bring rural produce to the railway which will carry it to markets and cities.

▲ Picking lychees, a sweet fruit.

◄ Workers at a cannery run by peasant households wash a crop of mushrooms. China exports canned produce to Japan, Southeast Asia, and western countries.

MODERN INDUSTRY

The Chinese economy is one of the largest in the world. In recent years emphasis has been on light industry, such as production of food, textiles, household appliances, and the assembly of computer components. State-owned enterprises are now expected to work efficiently and make a profit, while factories have been largely freed from bureaucratic control. Chinese people are contributing expertise gained from overseas study and employment, and businesses are developing projects in partnership with investors and advisors from other countries.

▲ A giant crane is part of heavy industrial equipment used on major construction projects. Before being able to advance its industry and technology, China has had to build an infrastructure—a system of basic requirements for modern industry, such as electricity and transport on waterways, railways, and roads.

▼ This pharmaceutical laboratory attracts foreign investment.

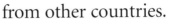

▲ Laborers still use hand tools
◀ for smaller jobs, but power tools are used on major construction.

▼ A nuclear power station under construction.

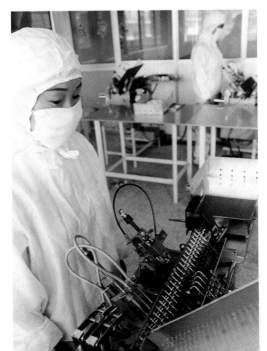

China is self-sufficient in oil and coal, the main energy source. It has built up its machinery, electronics, petrochemical, automobile, and construction industries. By developing its industries, China has increased food supply and housing. In their drive for more jobs, better pay, and a chance to get ahead, people put up with polluted air and water caused by industrial waste. The government is concerned with controlling pollution, as well as producing heating, food, and clothing for its population of 1.3 billion.

▲ Solar energy powers a television receiver in Tibet. Solar power does not pollute.

LIGHT INDUSTRY AND TEXTILES

The Chinese people are known as hard workers willing to spend many hours producing intricate items for sale. China is the world's number-one producer of bicycles, household pottery, and washing machines; second in raw salt, beer, and detergent; and third in paper and cardboard, watches, and freezers.

Clothing is sewn in homes and factories by quick, skillful operators who receive low wages. Many of their products are exported to western markets where shops sell track suits, jeans, and every kind of garment at moderate prices.

Jade, a semi-precious stone, has been highly valued by Chinese people for centuries. Skilled workers in factories hand-carve jade into many useful and decorative objects, from tiny cups and intricate jewelry to large sculptures.

▲ A steel mill production line moves red hot steel ingots, which will eventually be shaped into metal objects such as car bodies, train wheels, or giant cranes.

CHINA'S CITIES

Modern Beijing surrounds the Forbidden City, once the Imperial Palace. The Emperor's Dragon Throne was considered the center of the world. In front, Tiananmen Square is flanked by major government buildings and museums. The snake and tortoise symbolize the north and the city of Beijing.

China's largest cities are in the east, where they have access to the seaboard, communications networks, business, and industrial zones. Beijing is a serious place—the capital of China and the center of government, education, and science. For centuries it was invaded, burnt, rebuilt, and renamed. The first emperor called it "Yan"; to the Mongols it was "Khanbaliq"; and westerners knew it as "Peking" until *pinyin* spelling changed it to "Beijing." Its streets are jammed with thousands of bicycles, taxis, and carts. From early morning, shoppers stream to the markets, and workers leave their small rented flats for places of work or study. A million daily visitors make moving about very difficult.

◀ Beijing Opera, with its lavish costumes, has a long tradition.

▶ Traffic police direct the thousands of slowly moving cars and bicycles.

◀ The Shanghai flower market is especially busy at Chinese New Year.

▶ This street won an award in a "Clean Streets" campaign.

▼ Nanjing Road Shanghai is closed to traffic on Saturday evening, as "Walking Street."

Shanghai is situated on the coast, south of the Changjiang and, with 18 million people, is China's largest city and industrial and commercial center. Ships from its busy wharves go out to 300 ports worldwide. Growing rapidly through international trade, the city is constantly changing, with skyscrapers, modern department stores, neon lights, and multilane highways.

Hong Kong, under a century of British control, became a wealthy business center with many high-rise office blocks, international hotels, and a busy airport. It was peacefully returned to China in 1997.

▲ Hong Kong's triangular Bank of China tower was designed by international architect I M Pei.

▼ Pudong New Area, Shanghai, was farmland until 1990, when construction of a Special Economic Zone began.

◀ For many years low prices made Hong Kong a busy tourist and shopping center.

CONTINUITY AND CHANGE

In the last hundred years China has gone through great and rapid change. Many things altered after dynastic rule was overthrown by republican revolution, and later replaced by communism. But China is a country so big and so diverse that old ways of doing things often continue alongside the new. Traditions once central to a way of life are now more often seen as performances or depicted in museums. The communist view is that belief in God will "wither away," but many people still worship their ancient deities or follow other beliefs. The long battle against catastrophic floods continues with construction of the Three Gorges Dam, the world's largest water control project. Western technology has caught the imagination of the Chinese. Most city dwellers own a television set and refrigerator. Cars are a luxury, but motorcycles are common and popular with young people.

▲ The flat-bottomed *sampan* and the wooden junk have remained the same for centuries and are still common on China's waterways.

▶ This girl lives in Tibet, which was invaded by China in 1951. Now 460,000 Tibetans are Chinese citizens and one of its 55 different National Minorities.

▼ Nail guards were a sign of wealth and status in imperial times. The very long nails of the upper classes showed that their hands were never used in manual work.

▲ Trucks dumped loads of rock into a gap which dammed the main course of the Changjiang in 1977. It is planned that the Three Gorges Dam will be complete by 2009.

▶ Radical changes in the last hundred years have altered the role of women, who were once little valued. Girls now receive an education. Women have always worked hard, but now they can enter many different occupations. This woman is an engineer in charge of a section on the Three Gorges Dam construction site.

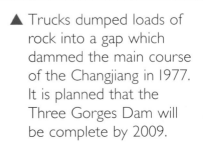

▲ An ancient way of buying and selling is still practiced in the countryside. A woman has set up a roadside stall simply by laying her carpet over the dust and setting her vegetables out for passing buyers. Children sleep warmly under another rug.

▶ China now allows private businesses within a state-controlled system. In Shanghai Friendship Commercial City large modern shopping complexes have been built in partnership with companies from other nations.

▲ Bicycles have been used to transport
◀ both people and goods around China for decades. Those who have cars can find filling stations even in isolated places.

◀ Acupuncture is an ancient method of treating pain by stimulating pressure points with very fine needles.

▶ On International Red Cross Day a Beijing woman donates blood at a street collection station. Western medicine has helped increase life expectancy from 35 to 71 years.

THE FAMILY

Family ties are very strong in Chinese society. Confucian rules made the family the center of organization with the father as head—a son obeyed his father, a woman her father or husband, and parents arranged their children's marriages. These strict rules no longer apply, but respect is shown. Adults now choose their own husbands or wives. The extended family includes grandparents, uncles, aunts, and cousins as part of a close-knit clan. They no longer all live in the same house or village but still like to keep in touch.

◀ Families are visited and gifts exchanged at Chinese New Year. Also called the Spring Festival, it is the most important celebration of the year.

▼ These Uygur people live in an arid part of Xinjiang Province. Children and animals share the wide, open spaces.

◀ Older people are respected for their wisdom. In many families grandparents live with their adult children and grandchildren. Often both parents work and children are left with their grandparents or at a child-care center.

▲ Sharing a meal with all the family is an important custom.

Children are the center of attention and greatly cared for. Traditionally families were large and the eldest or "Number One" son inherited the role of family leader, but now couples are limited to one child. Because it is still considered important to have a son to pass on the family name, many who have a girl want another child. Rural families and National Minorities are permitted more than one child.

During the 1970s population growth was so rapid that a government policy of one-child families offered cash bonuses, better housing, and medical care to parents who had only one child. Population increase has slowed, but now there are so many more young men than women that it is hard for them to find wives.

◀ Many single children are so pampered that they are known as "little emperors."

NAMES
Family names are carried by sons from one generation to the next. Women do not change their names when they marry, but children take the father's family name. There are basically only 100 common family names, derived from counties where everyone had the same clan name. Examples are Wong, Zhang, and Li. The family name is placed first (the reverse order to western countries).

HOMES
In old apartments families lived in one or two rooms, sharing bathrooms and kitchens. Modern apartments are being built in cities and large towns. Some families live in unusual homes—in Yanan province there are cave homes; south of Guilin are cool bamboo houses on stilts; and herdsmen in Inner Mongolia live as they have done for centuries in round, felt-covered *yurts*. In the north, houses are warmed by a *kang*—a raised platform of bricks heated by pipes leading from the stove, and padded with quilts.

▲ New high-rise apartments replace villages which will be submerged by the Three Gorges Dam.

◀ Families living close together in a village, street, or block of apartments make their own entertainment, as in this outdoor billiard game.

FOOD FROM FAR REGIONS

▲ Rice has been a basic food for thousands of years.

Endlessly different dishes combine red meat, fish, pork, and poultry with grains and plants grown in the varied climates and soils of China's regions. Generally, people in the north eat wheat, millet, and soy (as in steamed buns and noodles), while southern Guangzhou (Cantonese) dishes combine rice with abundant vegetables and fruit. Sichuan food is hot and spicy, while in the east, Shanghai cooks use oil. All are distinctive and delicious!

▲ The *wok* and bamboo steamer are basic cooking utensils throughout China. Small pieces of food are quickly stir-fried in oil or steamed in a bamboo basket over boiling water. These methods save fuel and retain nutrients, and the lightly cooked fresh vegetables and small amounts of meat make a healthy diet.

◀ A *wok* is easily used on a small outdoor fire to prepare steaming hot picnic food.

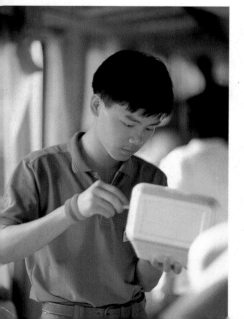

◀ Packaged fast food is sold at railway stations.

▶ Hot food and warmth make a street vendor welcome in wintry streets. Tea is a favorite drink, and hot water is available everywhere in vacuum flasks, even on trains.

Food is so important to the Chinese that their greeting *"Chi le ma?"* means "Have you eaten?" Families meet over a meal and may spend half their income on food. Ingredients are selected and balanced for taste, smell, and flavor and, just as important, for healthy body and mind.

▲ Wheat flour and lamb, products of the north, are cooked on the central stove of a Kazhak *yurt*.

◄ A weekend family reunion supper, when 78-year-old Beijing writer Wang Zenggi invites his children to taste his cooking.

▶ Exotic dishes, such as snake meat or bear's paw, are served in restaurants.

TABLE SETTINGS

- A table setting will include chopsticks, a bowl and porcelain spoon, a side plate, and sauce dishes.
- Each person chooses food from the main dishes and eats from the small bowls, dipping morsels in the sauces.
- There is no set order, although soup and rice are served as a later course, rather than first.
- Small cups of tea are served.

▲ *Dim sum*, small savories steamed or fried, are a favorite lunch.

▶ The noodle-maker tosses and twists his dough. Made from wheat or rice flour, noodles are boiled, used in soups, or fried in hot oil until crisp.

◄ A "bowl-dish" is shared.

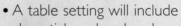

EDUCATION

Scholars were traditionally honored in China, and all officials were educated in the classics, but lower classes received no schooling. In the early 1900s, some new-style schools opened, and later the Communist Party aimed to make education available to all (but tried to destroy traditional knowledge). Now, education is given the highest priority, with emphasis on the training of future scientists, economists, and political leaders. The government has the mammoth task of supplying enough teachers and equipment for children all over China to have at least nine years of education and learn to speak the Chinese national language. Passing state examinations is the most important goal.

▲ Lower middle school pupils (age 13 to 16 years) learn history, geography, a foreign language (usually English), and sciences. Vocational schools offer practical courses such as agriculture and woodwork.

After school or work, children and adults can attend classes ranging from language or the arts to computer science.

▶ A student attends a Children's Palace to learn classical Chinese music, which is based on a different scale from western music.

▲ Learning to read and write Chinese takes a great deal of classroom time. Other elementary school subjects include mathematics, general knowledge, and political science. Children participate in dancing, singing, and sports such as martial arts, swimming, gymnastics, and team games including basketball and baseball.

▼ Three- to six-year-olds attend preschools.

▲ National minority students attend language centers to learn *putonghua* as their second language.

▲ Only 10 percent of applicants gain university and college entrance.

CHINESE LANGUAGE AND WRITING

There is a distinction between spoken and written Chinese—spoken Chinese varies between regions so much that one region often cannot understand another; the written language is the same for all.

• *Putonghua* was proclaimed the "common speech" of the People's Republic of China in 1955. In addition to sounds there are four different tones, or pitches, which give meaning to words. *Putonghua* is taught in schools, used in radio and television, and learned by foreigners.

• Written words are a combination of pictographs (pictures or symbols of objects), ideographs (pictures or symbols of ideas), and phonetic (or sound) characters.

• Basic literacy (sufficient to read a newspaper or magazine) uses up to 3,000 characters. A scholar would recognize some 10,000 out of about 50,000 characters in a large dictionary.

• *Pinyin* is a system that spells Chinese words with the roman letters used in English. A word processor transliterates words typed on a *pinyin* keyboard into Chinese characters, which can be seen on screen or printed.

▲ Stylized calligraphy character meaning "long life."

▶ Computer facilities in rural centers provide classes for isolated students.

VISITING CHINA

China's size, its grandeur, its multitudes of people and the choice of what to see can be overwhelming for visitors. In Beijing, cross the expanse of Tiananmen Square and enter the Forbidden City. Travel north to the Great Wall—to walk the entire length of the wall would take a whole year! Explore the eroded dome-shaped mountains of Guilin, and enter the maze of sharp rocks in the Stone Forest. See rows of terracotta warriors unearthed at Xian, visit the circus and markets of Shanghai, or travel by boat through the towering gorges of a great river. There is so much to see and do!

▲ You can walk the length of this corridor between the outer and inner walls of the Forbidden City.

▲ Old jewelery can be found in markets and antique shops

. . .and you can buy many goods from roadside vendors.
▼

▲ Minority groups in traditional costume perform music and dance.

◀ The zigzag bridge of Shanghai's Yuyuan Gardens in the old city.

▼ A footpath calligrapher will write your name in Chinese characters.

◀ Only a few bat-wing junks continue to ride the current of the mighty Changjiang.

◀ Travel overnight by "hard" sleeper train. Passengers sleep on the wooden seats or sit below to talk or play cards.

▼ A circus performer "tames" a wild panda. The Chinese circus is world famous.

▼ Instead of your soft pillow, try an antique ceramic headrest from Beijing's famous Theatre Arts Shop.

▲ Ride a camel across the sand dunes of the Gansu Desert, part of the ancient Silk Road.

▼ A summer reflection of Qomolangma (Mount Everest) —not for every tourist, but the ultimate challenge to the world's mountaineers.

INDEX

How to use the Index
Words in standard type are specific references.
Words in **bold** type are general subject references;
the word itself may not appear on each page listed.

PICTURE CREDITS

Abbreviations: r = right, l = left,
t = top, c = center, b = below

Mike Langford
Contents; **10** cl, bl, br; **11** cl, c, br; **12** br;
15 bl, br; **16** bl; **17** c, br; **18** c, b; **19** tr;
21 bl; **24** tl; **25** bl; **27** tl, tr, br; **30** cl, c, cr;
31 tl, cl; **32** cr; **33** c, bl; **34** br; **35** tc, tr;
36 tr; **37** tl, cr; **38** tl, cl, br; **39** bl, c, tr;
40 bl, br; **41** tr, cr; **42** tl, cr, br;
44 tl, cl, bl, cr; **45** tl, tc.

Xinhua News Agency
Introduction; **12** bl; **13** tr; **14** br; **15** tl,
tr; **16** tl; **26** tr; **27** c, bl; **28** tl, bl; **29** bl,
tr; **30** tl, b; **31** b; **32** tl, bl, c, br; **33** tr,
br; **34** tl; **35** br; **36** bl, br; **37** cl, br; **39**
br; **40** cl; **41** tl; **43** tl, tr, br.

Hong Kong Tourist Association
Cover, **9** br; **17** bl; **21** tr; **28** br; **29** tl, br;
31 tr; **34** bl; **35** bl, cr; **36** tl; **38** c; **41** bl,
c, br; **42** cl; **44** br.

Lynette Cunnington Asian Art
16 cr; **19** tl; **20** tl, bl, tr; **21** tl; **22** br;
29 c; **36** c; **39** tl; **43** cl.

Denny Allnutt
Title; **13** b; **17** c, tr; **19** br; **33** tl; **34** tr;
40 tl; **44** tr; **45** c.

China National Tourist Office
12 tr; **14** tl; **20** br; **31** cr; **35** tl; **37** tr;
44 c; **45** cr.

**Consulate-General of the
People's Republic of China**
13 l, c; **23** bl; **26** tl.

Valerie Hill
22 bl, bc; **28** cl.

Allan Ashby
37 bl; **38** bl.

AP/AAP
21 br; **25** r.

Auscape International
10 tl; **45** b.

Sovfoto/Eastfoto
23 tr; **24** br.

Garuda Indonesia
40 tr.

Pavel German
8 tl.

The Shanghai Museum
22 tl.

Peter Barker
18 tl; **19** bl (artwork).

Allen Roberts
22 tr; **23** br (artwork).

Ray Sim
8; **11** maps.

Every effort has been
made to consult all
relevant people and
organizations. Any
omissions or errors are
unintentional and should
be reported to Vineyard
Freepress Pty Ltd.